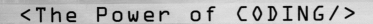

<The Power of CODING/>

The Power of C++

Ashley M. Ehman

Cavendish
Square
New York

Library of Congress Cataloging-in-Publication Data

Names: Ehman, Ashley.
Title: The power of C++ / Ashley Ehman.
Description: New York : Cavendish Square Publishing, 2018. | Series: The Power of coding | Includes bibliographical references and index.
Identifiers: LCCN ISBN 9781502634207 (pbk.) | ISBN 9781502629401 (library bound) | ISBN 9781502629418 (ebook)
Subjects: LCSH: C++ (Computer program language)--Juvenile literature. | Computer programming--Juvenile literature.
Classification: LCC QA76.73.C153 E46 2018 | DDC 794./1526--dc23

Editorial Director: David McNamara
Editor: Caitlyn Miller
Copy Editor: Rebecca Rohan
Associate Art Director: Amy Greenan
Designer: Christina Shults
Production Assistant: Karol Szymczuk

1 The History of C++. 5

2 How It Works 31

3 Strengths and Weaknesses 55

4 Getting Started with C++ 75

Glossary 100

Further Information 104

Bibliography. 106

Index 109

About the Author 112

The History of C++

T ake a look around you. Perhaps you are at home, reading this book in your room, or even at school, skimming these pages during your study period. You might see someone clicking away at a laptop, or a friend texting on their smartphone. Not so long ago, this would have been a much different picture. Instead of these modern conveniences, you would have seen people communicating on a large, bulky, desktop computer complete with clunky keyboard or a landline telephone. Yet, technology has a way of evolving—and expanding.

Opposite: The way that students learn in the classroom has been greatly influenced by modern technologies, such as laptop computers.

Aside from their physical appearances, the devices that you use are only as advanced as they are because of the computer programmers who gear them toward everyday people. A big part of emphasizing usability is creating effective coding languages that can adapt as technology does. One such adaptable language is C++.

Simula to C with Classes

Like the technology it drives, C++ had a somewhat complicated history before finally becoming the language we know it as today. As it stands, C++ is used in a variety of platforms and serves as the inspiration for many of the languages that were developed after it. Its status as a general-purpose programming language makes it useful in nearly every application that implements C++. This is because it can be adapted to fit the needs of the program. Where other languages specialize in particular programming tactics, C++ serves as a catchall in the programming community. While it was influenced by a lot of other programming languages, Simula 67 was the one that influenced C++ the most. Simula 67, or Simula for short, was a programming language created in the 1960s to run computer simulations. It is from this language that a programmer named Bjarne Stroustrup first began forming his main ideas of what C++ should be. During his time as a student at the Computing Laboratory

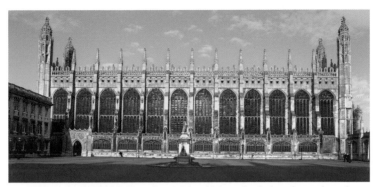

Bjarne Stroustrup studied at Cambridge University in London, where he learned a great deal about what he would eventually turn into C++.

of Cambridge University in London, Stroustrup became more and more familiar with Simula. One of the main things that stood out to him was the language's ability to map out his ideas into actual constructed code known as **classes**. Because of its use of classes, Simula was incredibly readable to the programmer. Classes also made Simula much easier to understand for those who were not familiar with a chunk of code's purpose.

Along with its easily understood **syntax** (the "grammar" of the code itself), the language also allowed for fewer errors to occur when the program began running, thanks to its ability to recognize type errors. A type error is when a program acts in an undesirable way. Type errors are due to an irresolvable difference between the kind of data being placed into the program and what the program is supposed to do with this data. Think of it this way: a raw egg and a hard-boiled egg are both eggs, but only one can make a cake. In this example, the egg is the variable (think of a variable as a container for storing data). The hard-boiled versus raw characteristic is its data type. Finally, the cake at the end of the process is the program. While Simula had strengths in its **zero-level abstraction** and ability to pick out type errors, Stroustrup saw that it also had its downfalls.

As he worked more and more with Simula, he noted a few things that were undesirable about the language. As his projects grew in size and scope, Stroustrup became increasingly more aware of Simula's inability to grow with his programs. When he asked his programs to communicate with separate classes, he ran into time issues. The time it took to run the programs was not as quick as it had been when his programs were smaller. In addition, he found that what is known as runtime performance was also poor. This meant that it was unrealistic to continue running simulations, as the data retrieved would be essentially useless. As a last-ditch effort to save his project, Stroustrup rewrote the entire thing using a more machine-oriented language called BCPL. The problems he'd encountered with Simula were so severe that if he had not rewritten his project, he would

Variables are like eggs. Even though they appear the same on the outside, the information, or yolk, that's contained within the shell is what makes the program run.

not have earned his PhD. His final project ran at speeds that were desirable. However, BCPL lacked the simplistic implementation that Simula had offered.

C is Born

Because of his time spent at Cambridge, Stroustrup saw a need for a new programming language. He hoped to combine zero-level abstraction with close proximity to hardware. The idea of proximity simply means that the physical elements that run the software would be those pieces that were closest to the main components of the machine it was running on. This became the basis for what would eventually be known as C++. From there, he determined that his language would have to be a suitable tool for program organization, run as fast as BCPL, and allow for portable implementations. Portable implementation is the idea that a program running on one computer could be brought to another computer and run in much the same fashion. At the time, there were a few options out there for such a language. The only problem? They were far from affordable for the casual programmer. Stroustrup imagined something that would be appealing to the expert and novice programmer alike. It was not until he began working at a company called Bell Laboratories, however, that his idea finally began to come to fruition.

Upon accepting his position at the Computer Science Research Center of Bell Laboratories in April of 1979, Stroustrup was tasked the job of analyzing the most recent UNIX **kernel,** or the core program that runs a computer's operating system. Much like his time spent with Simula and BCPL, he began to have issues with the language at hand, so he set out to design a tool that could adequately perform the tasks he asked of it.

By October of that same year, Stroustrup had managed to implement the necessary changes he wanted, using an existing language, known as C. Combining his need for organization and speed, he developed C with Classes. It was primarily viewed as an update to C, but this was a language all its own.

Bell Laboratories

○ ○ ○

Bell Laboratories has been the birthplace of many technologies, including those that use and influence C++.

The very beginnings of Bell Laboratories can be traced back to Alexander Graham Bell, who invented the telephone in 1876. Initially a part of the American Telephone and Telegraph Company, more commonly known as AT&T, Bell Labs has always been at the forefront of innovation. In fact, Bell Labs was originally known as the research department within Western Electric and served as one of the many **subsidiaries** that functioned under AT&T. Ultimately, AT&T (and Western Electric with it) decided to split its research from its normal business functions. This created a standalone research division, known as Bell Telephone Laboratories. The newly formed Bell Labs began operation on January 1, 1925. Continually growing between the 1930s and the 1970s, Bell Labs became the birthplace for many important technologies that we still use today.

Bell Laboratories (continued)

○ ○ ○

With the advent of World War II, Bell Laboratories saw an influx of military-based discoveries in the 1930s. These innovations included the two-way radio, the bazooka, and radar. Bell Laboratories even made it possible for Franklin Roosevelt and Winston Churchill to communicate securely from opposite sides of the Atlantic through machines called SIGSALY, enabling the Allied Forces to remain in near-constant contact. Because of these inventions, and the many other contributions scientists at Bell Laboratories made, research efforts continued to expand beyond the 1930s and into the late 1970s. The number of PC-based inventions created greatly increased in the 1970s and 1980s. C++ aside, the laboratories also saw ideas like the Unix Operating System come to fruition. In addition, researchers at Bell Labs pioneered fiber-optic technology. And in time, optical fiber would be used to keep the world connected, thanks to the invention of the internet. But Bell Laboratories eventually faced tremendous setbacks.

Due to allegations that AT&T was in violation of the United States's antitrust law, the company was taken to court in 1984. During the hearing, they were determined to be a monopoly within the communications industry. The courts required that AT&T remove itself from any local telephone operations it was a part of, and Bell Laboratories was affected. Bell Labs continued to exist, but the smaller-scale business operations meant there were fewer financial resources to pull from. Their research endeavors shrank. Met again with difficulties in 1996, AT&T completely severed ties with Bell Laboratories and instead placed them under the control of

Routers are among the many devices that have been imrpoved by Lucent Technologies.

Alcatel-Lucent Corporation. While Lucent Technologies was smaller than the original Bell Laboratories were back during their prime, Lucent Laboratories still funded research endeavors within the voice and data communications sector. The most recent change of hands took place in 2015, when Nokia merged with Alcatel-Lucent in a $17 billion deal. Today, Lucent Technologies focuses on developing elements that help enable telecommunication. This includes making better routers, switches, and cables. Since its creation in the early 1900s, Bell Laboratories has seen more than ten Nobel Prize winners and hundreds of inventions pass through its doors. Regardless of what name it was functioning under, Bell Labs has made an unmatchable contribution to the telecommunication industry.

How C with Classes Became C++

C with Classes received mildly positive support from the programming community, and Stroustrup was left with a choice. Should he give up on C with Classes and do something else with his time? Or should he develop an even better language that would have a greater amount of potential and support? Thankfully, Stroustrup made the latter decision. After analyzing the weaknesses of his initial attempt, C with Classes, he determined that its successor needed to be more streamlined. In addition, it had to be implemented using compiler technology that was more accessible to a large range of people.

With an entirely new coding language in the works, Stroustrup maintained a few key questions throughout the initial design process of C++:

1. Who would its users be?
2. What kinds of hardware would they be using?
3. How would he leave the business of making tools to instead make a successful language?
4. How should the above answers affect how he defined the language?

While his questions seemed simple enough, their answers were far from it.

Much like any other product on the market, the first question Stroustrup had was who would be using his program. Without a viable audience, his efforts would not pay off. Initially, he pinpointed his audience to be himself and fellow colleagues at Bell Laboratories. He and his colleagues were in desperate need of a programming language that did what Stroustrup promised. From there, Stroustrup hoped that its use would spread to AT&T and eventually on to universities. The process would end with it finally reaching beyond that to a point where AT&T could make money by selling the evolved set of tools that came from his language. Stroustrup set out to work with affordability in mind, reasoning that bigger corporations, like AT&T, could create more industrialized versions of his language that met their needs. After all, cost was hardly a concern for large, well-established corporations. It was in this way that Stroustrup managed to leave the business of making tools, answering the third question he had posed in his language-making process. By putting the responsibility of advancement on someone other than himself, Stroustrup was able to let C++ form into whatever its users needed at the time, since it was they themselves who would be molding it to their needs.

Another important element of C++'s design Stroustrup had to consider was the type of system it would be used on. Since his language was heavily influenced and modeled after C with Classes, he determined that it should run on many of the same systems. Since C with Classes was an incredibly portable language at the time, it was Stroustrup's intention for C++ to run on anything from supercomputers to the most basic systems. Thus, C++ had to be able to be run on variable amounts of memory. This included memory sizes from large to miniscule, leaving no room to assume the size and the speed of the machines that were in use. Stroustrup considered these and other technical aspects as he moved forward. The final piece of defining the language was deciding on a compiler. Stroustrup determined that C++ could not require a super-sophisticated compiler. Knowing that he needed a simple compiler in order for his language to execute in the fashion he desired, Stroustrup took matters into his own hands and made the CFront compiler a reality.

The CFront Compiler

Before delving into the details of Stroustrup's CFront compiler, it is important to understand what a compiler does on a basic level. Compilers fill an essential role in implementing programming languages. This is due to the fact that compilers serve as a means of translation for the machine that is generating the code. There are three parts to the compilation process, which is a simple execution of inputs and outputs. The user codes and designs the source program using a source language, or language that can be read and understood by the programmer. In the case of the CFront compiler, the source language being used is C++. The source language serves as the version of the program that is defined by human concepts. Once inputted into the compiler, the compiler then checks for errors within the source code. These errors can span any of the following categories: syntax, semantics (the meaning of strings of code), and code generation. It is because of this error-checking ability that compilers are a vital component in the debugging process. Once a program compiles without triggering any errors, the compiler then translates the human-readable code into an assembly language, or language that the machine itself can make sense of. Upon successful compilation, the program is then implemented and executes the task being asked of it, barring any runtime errors.

With the initial design stages of C++ complete, Stroustrup turned his attention to creating a compiler devoted to making the most out of his language. First available in 1983, the CFront compiler was designed with simplicity in mind. Knowing that people were resistant to change, Stroustrup made it so his compiler would translate the inputted C++ source program into machine-generated C language. This was a good choice because it allowed those who were familiar with the "old" C language to still maintain a certain familiarity with how their programs worked. In addition, technology at the time did not support C++ **debuggers**. The lack of a debugger forced programmers to look for errors in their C-generated machine code. While this was tedious, it did not deter people from using C++ since C was already a commonly understood language within the computer science industry. Lastly, and potentially the most influential, was the CFront compiler's ability to transfer to new platforms. Because it broke down C++ into C, the CFront compiler could be placed on any system that housed a C compiler. At the time, a C compiler could be found on nearly every machine in use.

CFront was unique in the sense that it was one of the first front-end compilers, meaning that instead of having one compilation process, C++ required two. Initially, the C++ source program would be compiled and then translated into a C-based machine language. That in turn would then be placed within the resident C compiler, which would be the one to actually execute the code upon completion. Stroustrup made this decision because C was a common input format within the user community in the 1980s, and he found that creating a standalone compiler for C++ was not what users needed. Because C++ was designed to integrate with the more traditional compiler technologies of the time, CFront's last implementation was released in 1993; newer compilation technologies have paved the way into the twenty-first century.

Why Use C?

With all the other languages in use at the time, one might ask why Stroustrup decide to base his own language off of C, instead of some other programming language. The simplest answer is that Stroustrup had a background of knowledge in C, since he spent much of his time in school using that language. However, there are a few key characteristics of C that made it a desirable model to base his own language off of. The first one was its availability. Most every device in use at the time had a C compiler available. If for some reason it did not, there was often a multitude of resources to pull from so that a programmer hardly ever had to design a new compiler system from the ground up. In conjunction with its availability, C was also portable. While it was not immediately possible to transfer a C program from one computer to another, it was practical both technologically and financially to make this happen with the right software. The last two key components that contributed to using

C as a basis for C++ was its flexibility and efficiency. Stroustrup had wanted to design a program that could be used by a large audience on a variety of projects. Therefore, he needed a language that would adapt to each user's unique needs, while still matching the memory constraints that they had placed upon them. Even though it was modeled after C, Stroustrup wanted C++ to be seen as a new program entirely, which caused problems during the naming process.

How C++ Got Its Name

While it is known ubiquitously throughout the computer science community today as C++, Stroustrup's programming language went through many name changes before arriving at its current name. When development began in 1983, the resulting programming language was still known as C with Classes. Confusing, right? The language underwent its first name change at the request of one of Stroustrup's managers at Bell Laboratories, at which point it became known as C84. These changes helped break the habit of people referring to the different versions of C with Classes as the "new C" and the "old C," since they no longer shared a name. However, this new identity as C84 lasted mere months before another name change was suggested.

While the name C84 alleviated confusion between the varying C with Classes conundrum, it created further confusion because of the number following the C. It was often common when naming coding languages to incorporate the year they were **standardized**. By these means, its current name gave the appearance that C was standardized in 1984. This was not true. In addition to this logic, C84 was not an attractive name. It lacked appeal to the everyday programmer because it sounded too institutional. The final name change to C++ was suggested by Rick Mascitti and formally put into use in December of 1983. Stroustrup chose this name because it was simple and lacked any sort of indication that it was a new variety of the same "old" C language. This was because the "plus plus" (as it stands in the coding community) was interpreted to mean "successor" or "next." Though it was quite a process to settle on its current name, "C++" cleared up a lot of confusion within the programming community.

What Problems C++ Solved

C++ brought a lot of desirable features to the field of computer science. Quite possibly one of the most important ideas that drove the evolving C++ language forward was the fact that it was motivated by real problems. Programmers wanted a tool that could be shaped to fit their needs. This tool had to allow them to focus on the task at hand, instead of trying to fit their task into their available resources. This need was articulated in C++'s general-purpose language design. In being a general-purpose language, C++ could be used in a wide array of applications. This kind of flexibility usually makes a language more complicated, but Stroustrup's decision to compartmentalize his language helped keep things simple. A programmer did not have to understand every class that was within the C++ library.

Another problem that was addressed by C++ was the lack of **abstraction** available in other languages at the time. Abstraction is the idea that only the relevant data should be shown. Therefore, any excessive complexities were below surface-level, making way for new and interesting implementation techniques. It also allowed C++ the freedom to eliminate type violations, since users were allowed to formulate their own **data structures**. While this introduced potential security threats, Stroustrup found that the increased flexibility outweighed the risk. Virtual **functions** allowed for a class to define the general properties of an **object**. From there, more specific objects could be made. For example, a programmer could create a class named "Vehicle," which would house information such as whether or not the vehicle in question was a sedan, truck, or SUV. From there, a more specific class of type "Vehicle," such as class "Truck" could be created to house Make, Model, and Year. The increased lack of security came from the fact that most of these classes were to remain public, or open to threats. However, this allowed C++ to meet more people's needs and become increasingly appealing to a variety of users.

Lastly, Stroustrup's ability to recognize the need for an affordable option drew users to his programming language. He set out to design a language that could be implemented by even the poorest graduate students, since it was created with portability in mind. Stroustrup had successfully designed a language and compiler that could be run on the IBM PC/AT. At the time, the IBM computer had a mere 16 MB of memory. (To put that into perspective, today's average

C++ was able to run on IBM's PC/AT computer, which had very little available memory to run such a program. This made C++ useful to many people.

computer user has anywhere between 4 and 6 gigabytes of memory available. That is an increase of 375 percent!) At the time of creation, memory constraints were not as important since the available technology did not allow for everyday people to program. Unfortunately, the available machines were still clunky and expensive. However, the PC revolution brought computers into a growing number of American households by the late 1980s, and the expanded adoption of computers became an important element of C++'s growth. This growth even garnered the attention of commercial software developers.

C++ Today

C++ as we know it today is hardly the same beast as Stroustrup's 1983 creation. The language has undergone many changes and updates to adapt to monumental changes in computing. However, C++ is still an active and widely used language among programmers worldwide.

The Influence of C++

Quite possibly the largest influence C++ has had is in the realm of **object-oriented programming (OOP)**. While it was introduced as a general-purpose programming language, C++ was the first of its kind to lend itself to successful object-oriented design. At the time of its creation, C++ challenged two universal "truths": 1) OOP was inefficient and messy, and 2) OOP could be used only by expert programmers due to its extreme complexity.

Because of its ability to overcome these obstacles, C++ heavily influenced other OOP languages to come, forcing the coding community to accept object-oriented programs as a useful tool. Nods to C++ can be found in Java, C#, and many other popular languages used today. Aside from the languages it has helped to shape, C++ can be found in a number of applications that millions of people use on a daily basis.

Due to its overwhelming popularity, C++ influences a variety of systems and programs. However, it is often difficult to document where it is currently being used. This is because there is no centralized C++ organization that tracks this information. C++ was and still is distributed commercially for industries to use as they please, meaning their implementations don't need to be released publicly. Even though its detailed usage is usually hidden from view, C++ can be found in anything from e-commerce, such as Amazon, to popular design programs, such as Adobe's Photoshop and Illustrator. From there, some of the language's more interesting applications include games, such as Halo and StarCraft, and entertainment like the Apple iPod's **interface**.

After becoming standardized for the first time in 1998, C++ solidified its presence in the future of programming. In doing so, a committee was appointed to manage subsequent releases of the language. The committee also determined what new features would be implemented in the new editions. The committee's role helped the language become more mainstream, and the organization has since released three more standards. C++03, C++11, and C++14 were released in 2003, 2011, and 2014, respectively. With a staggering number of suggested **extensions** to be evaluated for future standards, there are tentative plans to release new versions in late 2017 and 2020. Some of the expected features intend to add mathematical special functions and include the ability to define an object as optional. In addition, a future edition will include the option to remove obsolete functions.

While other coding languages that were developed in the same timeframe as C++ have since grown outdated, C++ continues to improve and prove its worth to the programming community. The language has adapted to modern hardware and techniques quickly and efficiently. And Stroustrup, who has always put users first, still very much has a say in the direction C++ will go. He recognizes that new features are always a need. However, without **backwards compatibility** to use what has already been developed, his programming language would go from a tool that solved a problem to a headache for those who implemented old code.

Of course, a big part of the staying power of C++ is that Stroustrup developed it with both experts and novices in mind. He did not set out to design code to solve a particular problem. Rather, he designed C++ so that the programmer could make it into what he or she needed. This means even novice programmers can find uses for C++. With implementations spanning many industries, it looks like C++ has what it takes to last.

Bjarne Stroustrup

○ ○ ○

Bjarne Stroustrup (*left*) still works tirelessly to ensure C++ meets users' needs.

Born in Denmark on December 30, 1950, Bjarne Stroustrup is best known for creating the popular programming language C++. He attended Aarhus University until 1975, when he earned his master's degree in computer science. After graduation, his desire to learn more about distributed systems led him to pursue a PhD at the Computing Laboratory of Cambridge University in England, which he completed in 1979. It was during this period that he met and married his wife, Marian, and they welcomed a baby named Annemarie. After his studies at Cambridge came to an end, the entire family immigrated to New Jersey. Once there, he joined the Computer Science Research Center of Bell Telephone Laboratories.

During his time at Bell Laboratories, Stroustrup focused heavily on the development of C++ and made his idea a reality. He and his wife also welcomed a son named Nicholas while living in Meyersville, New Jersey. Following the various breakups of Bell Laboratories,

Stroustrup served as the department head for the Large-Scale Programming Research department until late 2002, when he joined the Computer Science department at Texas A&M University. During his time at the university, he served as the College of Engineering Chair in Computer Science. He served as a professor at the university until January 2014; he then moved to New York City to become the managing director in the technology division of Morgan Stanley. Stroustrup noted that academia can often distract from solving industrial problems, which was what C++ was made for in the first place. The relocation also allowed him to be closer to his daughter and son, who were by then working as a medical doctor and a professor in systems biology, respectively. Living in New York City also had the benefit of bringing him near to his grandchildren.

In addition to the various professional positions he has held over the years, Stroustrup has kept busy with many side projects and extracurriculars. He has written several books, including *The Design and Evolution of C++*, *The C++ Programming Language*, and *A Tour of C++*. Along with his writing projects, he remains an active participant in the **standardization** of the upcoming versions of C++.

Strostrup has received high honors within the computer science industry, including the Grace Murray Hopper award in 1993 and the Sigma Xi's William Procter Prize for Scientific Achievement in 2005. More recently, in October 2011, he was appointed to the board of directors for a cloud computing startup called RollApp. Still not busy enough for his liking, Stroustrup also secured a visiting professor position at Columbia University. He continues to publish academic research and papers and present them to the programming community. Nowadays, he focuses his research on areas involving design, performance, reliability, and distributed systems.

How It Works

L earning to code is much like the process of learning to drive a car. No one simply climbs in the front seat and drives off. New drivers must first become familiar with the basics of the vehicle. Is it a manual or automatic? Where's the shifter? Is visibility good, or should the mirrors be adjusted?

Similarly, novice coders need to learn the main ideas and concepts of a programming language in order to know how to effectively use it. C++ is no exception. This chapter looks at these concepts, as

Opposite: Just like driving a car, learning to code is easier when you know how all the different parts work.

well as common applications for C++, problems C++ can be used to solve, and the basics of the language.

Object-Oriented Programming

C++ is a general-purpose programming language, which means it takes on various aspects of other programming language types. Assembly languages, dataflow languages, and concurrent languages are all examples of programming language types, just to name a few. The most prevalent type, however, that C++ incorporates is object-oriented programming, or OOP for short. C++ was initially influential because it introduced the possibility of using objects with the implementation of an older language, such as C.

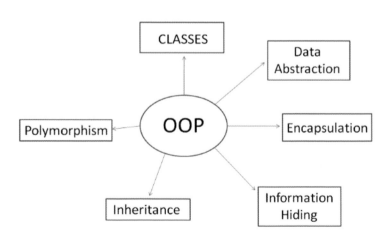

Object-oriented programming has a few key characteristics, including encapsulation, data abstraction, and classes.

While object-oriented design offers a multitude of advantages, there are a few in particular that make it better than other language choices. The first advantage it offers is data abstraction. Data abstraction is what allows a programmer to create classes in the first place. These classes are then used to make objects. (Think back to the cake analogy made in chapter 1). In turn, programmers are able to think about their program executions differently. Instead of relying on actions and logic, programmers are able to think of more concrete ideas like objects and data to achieve programmatic goals. Data abstraction is a more natural way to think when coding. It goes hand-in-hand with the next benefit of object-oriented programming: data encapsulation.

Data encapsulation is what allows the programmer to control what the user sees, datawise. Controlled access keeps various aspects of an object's data secure. In this way, data encapsulation prevents important data's integrity from being compromised. To fully grasp this concept, imagine the process of building a house for a new homeowner. The homeowner will communicate with the contractor about what they want their house to look like. Then the contractor will talk to their workers about how to accomplish the task. The contractor is aware of the different requirements, but that does not mean that the homeowner and workers need to know everything about the project. The workers do not need to be bothered with what color the front door is supposed to be, because they will not be the ones purchasing the materials. Similarly, the homeowner does not need to be informed about how many foremen are assigned to their house, only that they are meeting the deadlines set in place. Data encapsulation functions the same way; it keeps things on a need-to-know basis.

This need-to-know basis can be divided into three different levels of protection, based on how each class within a program is defined. The lowest level of protection comes with a public class, meaning that the data housed within the object class can be accessed by any other part of the program. The highest level of security can be found in a private object class. Only **methods**, or calculations, executed within that class can access the information. Sandwiched between the two is the protected object class. In a protected object class, information within the object cannot be accessed by every part of the program. However, this information can be used by other classes that inherit the traits of that class. This leads us into another valuable piece of object-oriented design, which is inheritance.

Inheritance is when a new class takes on the various traits and information of another class that it is based on. The original class or classes is known as the superclass or parent class. The newly produced class that receives the traits of the parent is called the child class. Inheritance allows for code to be reused, thus allowing the program to avoid repetitive code that is unnecessary to the function of the program. Inheritance can be either single or multiple in nature. Put simply, a child class can either have a single parent class, or more than one, which is called multiple inheritance. This hierarchy within a program is comparable to what a family tree would look like, which is why it is called inheritance.

The last item that object-oriented programming brought to C++ is the ability to use polymorphism within its code. Polymorphism allows a single function to be used in a variety of ways, based on the type of data that is being put into the calculation. Let's look at a simple adding function, for example. If a method, or calculation, is supposed to add two things together, it will need to act differently for numbers than it does for letters. Polymorphism techniques would allow the programmer to have one method of "Add" that handles words, while another adds numbers. When the program is asked to put two things together, it will then determine what data type is being added and then execute the function that accommodates the given types. Now that we've seen the pieces of object-oriented design, we'll turn to the various aspects that go into C++ itself.

Driving the C++ Machine: What Makes Up Its Parts

From variables to constants, numbers to letters, C++ can accommodate nearly any problem that it is given, so long as it is given the data in the correct fashion.

Variables

At a very basic level, the first thing a program will handle is the input of some sort of variable and its associated data. Similar to variables discussed in math classes, a variable in computer science is used in place of something else. The programmer will name their variable with some sort of identifier, and then it may be used to house data that is either known or unknown to the user. Within C++, there are four different variable types available for use.

The first variable type is called a Boolean, which is defined by placing "bool" before the identifier, or name of the variable. A Boolean can only house two options: true or false. This is how Booleans are used for flags within programs, or to determine when something should be done or not. For example, imagine a program

Boolean variables can be thought of as either "True" or "False."
No other piece of information is placed within them.

has a Boolean variable named "Stomach_Full" that is set to false. "Stomach_Full" is then sent through the method "Feed_Stomach" within which another variable called, "Food_Amount" is increased by one. The only way to prevent the "Stomach_Full" variable from being sent into the "Feed_Stomach" method is for the person eating to be full, which would then set "Stomach_Full" from false to true. In other words, a Boolean is like a light switch within the program; it is either on or off.

Another variable type that can be used is called a char, which only accepts a single letter at a time, otherwise known as a character. Characters are defined by either "char" or "wchar_t" when being initialized (when the variable is first mentioned within the program and is used to place any known data within said variable). "Char" is used for standard characters, which only require one byte of memory. "Wchar_t" is used for more complex characters that require two bytes of memory. An example of these more complex characters are Unicode characters, things such as #, $, and &, and any other character that does not belong to the standard "A through Z" alphabet. A char variable would be useful in a program that acted as a multiple-choice question. With a variable of type "char" named "User_answer," the user would simply input "A," "B," "C," or "D." The program could then compare it to another char variable, called "correct_answer" and then tell the user whether they were correct or not.

The next set of variables that are useful within C++ are those falling under the integral types category, which includes short, int, and long variables. Integral variables are used to house whole numbers of various lengths and are dependent on the amount of memory required. From smallest to largest amount of memory, short, int, and long variable usage is determined by the functions of the machine the program is being implemented on. If the computer has a smaller bit operating system, and thus contains less memory capacity, it would be beneficial to use numbers that are defined as shorts. Operating systems of today, however, are designed to easily accommodate int and long variables.

Much like integral types, floating point types also deal with numerical values. There's only one difference between integral and floating point types: floating point types are more specifically used for decimal numbers. Floating point types include variables defined as float, double, and long double. Which one should be used is determined by the amount of accuracy a programmer requires out of their program. The longer the decimal used, the more accurate the calculation. However, longer decimals also require more memory space, which is why there is not a single type of float point variable. Float is used for a normal amount of accuracy, whereas long double is used when accuracy is extremely important, leaving double to fall somewhere in the middle of these two.

Lastly, the final variable type worth discussing here is the string variable, which may bring images of yarn and twine to mind. Although the name implies something that can be tied, this variable is used to house words or sentences. By putting the type "string" in front of an identifier, it can then be used to hold extended amounts of words or phrases. This is useful in communicating with a program's user for a variety of reasons. If they enter information incorrectly, the string variable could be used to inform them of their error. For example, if the program wants a birthday in numerical "dd/mm/yyyy" format, and they enter "May 25, 2002," a string named "birthday_error" could be displayed on the screen, reading, "That birthday you have entered is incorrect. Please enter the birthday in dd/mm/yyyy format." Having discussed the different types of variables, the next important piece of C++ programming lies in its use of constants.

Constants

Similar to the basic premise behind variables, constants share many of the same traits and defining features as their variable counterparts. However, the difference is that constants are designed to contain the same value throughout the entire execution of the program. This value can be used within methods and calculations; however, the information that the constant holds does not change at any point. Constants are broken down into the same categories as variables, so we'll take a less-detailed look at them. However, below is a list of each data type and how a constant would be useful in an implementation that uses that type:

- Boolean constants: Boolean constants are used if there is not any case where something would change from true to false or vice versa. This type of constant would be useful in a program that explores fire, since a Boolean constant named "fire_burns" would always be set to true.

- Numerical constants: Numerical constants are utilized when a number does not change. For example, the freezing point of water is always 0 degrees Celsius, so a numerical constant named "freezing_point" would prove useful.

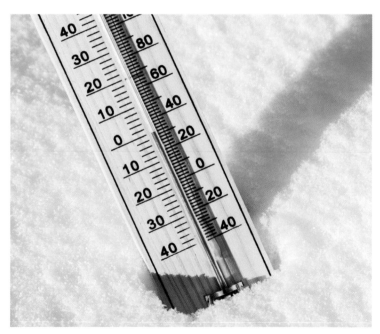

Numerical constants can be thought of as numbers that will never change, such as the freezing point of water.

- Character constants: Character constants are executed with a program where a letter does not change, such as the "correct_answer" variable discussed in the example above with char variables. In a multiple-choice question, the correct answer would never change, so a character constant that housed the correct answer to a question would be beneficial.
- String constants: String constants are implemented when a collection of words or phrases does not change. This would be useful in a program that returns a character's signature phrase, as that would never change. For example, if this program was asked to return the signature phrase of Bugs Bunny, it would read, "What's up, Doc?"

Constants can be very useful in the execution of a program. However, there are more things worth considering beyond variables and constants, which is the incorporation of control and special characters.

Bases? This Isn't Baseball!

○ ○ ○

C++ is able to accommodate a range of variables, but what about numbers that do not follow a base-10 numbering system? The standard numbering system we use is based on ten numbers. Listed out, they are 0, 1, 2, 3, 4, 5, 6, 7, 8, and 9. Any number within the system is made up of those ten. For C++ users, there are sometimes instances when the need to use base 8 or base 16 arises. These octal and hexadecimal numbers are easily incorporated through integral constants. Yet there's a special process for these numbers as they are not part of our standard numbering system.

Examine base 8, for example. The numbers that make up the base-8 notation are 0, 1, 2, 3, 4, 5, 6, and 7. It does not seem that different, right? Just like the numbering system most individuals are used to, counting works the same way. Starting with the smallest

Numbering systems aside from the standard base-10 system are often used in coding a variety of things, like video games.

Bases? This Isn't Baseball! (continued)

○ ○ ○

number, the numbers are counted up. Once 9 is reached in the standard numbering system, we move to the tens place and repeat the cycle of numbers. With this logic in mind, counting out base 8 would go as follows: 0, 1, 2, 3, 4, 5, 6, 7, 10, 11, 12, 13, 14, 15, 16, 17, 20 and so on. Because the octal number line does not allow for 8 or 9, they are simply omitted from the counting process. Base 16 works in much the same way, however that number line is as follows: 0, 1, 2, 3, 4, 5, 6, 7, 8, 9, A, B, C, D, E, F. The letters may seem a tad boggling, but when you think of them as additional numbers, it is easier to see that hexadecimal runs by the same logic as the octal and base-10 numbering system! While it may be confusing initially, different base notations are easily understood when written out.

Special Characters

Special characters are not used to hold information; rather, they are used to format the data that have been placed within the program. Special characters give programmers the control to display their program's information in a pleasing and readable fashion. These characters incorporate the use of a backslash (\). Referred to as an escape sequence, this backslash tells the program that the next character in the code is going to tell it how to display something. Common uses of special characters are combining the backslash with a "t," "n," or set of quotations. Backslash "t," or "\t," is used to represent a tab. Programming languages do not simply allow for the programmer to hit the tab button. Rather, they are forced to put phrases like this within their code to get the desired effect. When used alone, a standard "\t" represents eight consecutive spaces but can be changed to be any amount of spaces. If it is combined with other tab characters, it will align the consecutive information so that it lines up on the left side. The next common special character is backslash "n," or "\n." This is used to tell the program that the programmer would like the following information to be entered down onto the next line. Again, programs will not recognize an "Enter" keystroke like a word-processing software would. Rather, it views it as a way for the code itself to be more readable to the programmer, and thus concatenates the two separate lines upon program execution. (Concatenate means to form two string elements that are separated by white space into one string.) Lastly, a programmer will use the combination of a backslash with either a single quote or double quotation mark, " \'" or " \"" to display quotes within their information. Since quotation marks are used to tell the program what text is to be housed in a variable, if this was not done, the program would simply read it as an extra quote and disregard it.

While it may not initially seem like it, these characters are extremely useful in the programming community. They help display things in a readable, cohesive format and allow the user to better understand the program as a whole. Take the following program code for example:

```
"Chicken Nuggets Eaten this Week\n Monday:\t5\
nTuesday:\t12\nWednesday:\t34\nThursday:\t \"I
wasn't hungry.\"\nFriday:\t68"
```

This code isn't very easy for a person to read. One of the many jobs of the programmer is to make sure their program makes sense. By incorporating these special characters, they ensure that their information reads like any other line of text would to a person. Here's what this code would look like to the user once the program executed:

Displayed Information:
Chicken Nuggets Eaten this Week
Monday: 5
Tuesday: 12
Wednesday: 34
Thursday: "I wasn't hungry."
Friday: 68

The second one is a lot easier to understand, right? Without special characters, this information would appear as a jumbled mess to whoever was using the program. In having the programmer thoroughly understand the tools available to them, they are better prepared to design an effective program that the user can understand.

A Glance at a Basic Program

With a basic understanding of what goes into a C++ program out of the way, it's time to examine how the pieces actually form into a usable program. The first program nearly everyone codes in any programming language is known as "Hello World." Outlined below is the C++ version of this simplistic program:

```
// my first program in C++
#include <iostream>

int main()
{
    std::cout << "Hello World!";
}
```

Line by line, the program should be understood as follows:

- Line 1: This first line is a comment within the program. It does not affect the execution, nor is it displayed at any point. It is simply there to provide clarification to the programmer. Oftentimes, comments are used to outline what a particular method does, so that if someone other than the original programmer uses the code, they will understand how it works. Comments are always preceded by a set of forward slashes, with the entire comment displaying in a green color.

- Line 2: This is known as a **directive**. Directives are used by the preprocessor, which ensures that the program has the necessary resources from the C++ library to run. In this case, it is including the code from "iostream," which has already been developed and is being used here to display the phrase "Hello World!"
- Line 3: This is a blank line, simply included for easier readability. It does not affect the program.
- Line 4: This line declares "main" as a function of the program. Typically, programs run all of their major pieces from within a function named "main." It serves as the workplace of the program.
- Lines 5 and 7: These are the brackets that tell the program where a function begins and ends. Everything included within them is a part of the "main" function.
- Line 6: The meat of the program. The line begins with the C++ print function, known as "std::cout," which stands

for standard character output device.
This determines that the programmer
is (typically) displaying the following
information to a computer screen.
The words in quotes are what is to
be displayed. Then, like every line of
completed code, it ends with a semicolon.

When executed correctly, this program will display
as follows:

Hello World!

While this program is extremely simplistic, it is a
great starting point into more complicated endeavors
that benefit our lives every day.

C++ has a multitude of applications, but video game code is one of its
most common uses.

Everyday Applications

It may not be obvious, but C++ is a critical part of a variety of different platforms. Any time a user opens Photoshop, they have experienced the direct result of C++ **scripting**. When someone Googles cat pictures, they have, too: C++ is incorporated into Google's search engine code. Almost 99 percent of executable games utilize C++, so it even enables gaming. C++ can be found in anything from medical software to operating systems and is continually used in new applications. Yet, while it is an extremely useful programming language, it does have its strengths and weaknesses.

Self-Driving Cars

○ ○ ○

Exciting technological advances are made every day, and any number of these inventions and discoveries could change the way the world functions forever. Self-driving vehicles are one such invention that has tight ties with the programming community. And a new conglomerate known as Waymo is continually working toward making these cars a reality.

Beginning in 2009, Google began its self-driving car project. The initial goal was to equip a collection of Toyota Prius vehicles so that they were able to drive autonomously over a distance of 100 miles (160.9 kilometers). Three years later, they had accomplished that and more. Google began adding Lexus vehicles to their fleet and even allowed Google employees to test the technology on the road. While these cars were initially driven on freeways, Google moved to city streets later in 2012. The new, busy terrain introduced a whole new level of complexity. Having conquered these additional complications, Google released a new prototype vehicle in 2014 and put it to work on public roads in 2015. Since then, over two million miles have been traversed by self-driving vehicles. These self-driving cars utilize C++ to make it all happen.

Initially scripted with C++, these vehicles are now able to navigate four-way stops, predict what human drivers will do, and respond to emergency vehicles. The technology Waymo has developed is so advanced that the company even completed their first successful fully self-driven car ride in October of 2015, complete with passenger named Steven Mahan. Not only did the vehicle lack any sort of functional steering equipment or pedals, but Steven rode solo without assistance from a test driver. But that's not the exceptional part; the fact that Steven is legally blind is. The potential for self-driving vehicles offers enormous benefit to people like Steven, the elderly, and to everyone else. It is technology like this that could give people more freedom while providing a greater amount of safety on the road.

In addition to giving people the ability to go places without driving themselves, this developing technology will also provide a brand-new array of jobs. The number of people that is needed to develop, test, and fabricate these kinds of vehicles is astounding. Self-driving cars will strengthen the need for software engineers of all varieties, from those focusing on **embedded systems** to individuals who specialize in hardware. Along with jobs, Waymo hopes to make roads safer.

With nearly 94 percent of crashes being caused by human error in the United States, there is plenty of room for improvement. By taking the human part out of the driving equation, there is less likelihood of fatal accidents. Self-driving vehicles could replace drivers who speed, drink, text, or fall asleep at the wheel. At its core, Waymo would not be able to make this happen without the use of C++. It is applications like this that prove just how useful C++ remains and how it will usher in new technologies in the years to come.

<Chapter Three/>

Strengths and Weaknesses

As is the case with many technologies, there is always something better suited to tackle the task at hand. Photoshop is better suited to edit pictures than Microsoft Paint. Microsoft Word would be a better choice for writing an essay than Adobe Illustrator would be. With this idea in mind, there are also certain languages that are more effective at handling particular tasks. C++ may be a highly adaptable language, but even so, it has its own set of strengths and weaknesses.

Opposite: Just like athletes have strengths and weaknesses, C++ is better at some things than others.

Strengths of C++

As a general-purpose programming language, C++ has an extensive amount of beneficial features and a wide set of uses. The overall performance that C++ allows for might be its most important quality. Because C++ incorporates C into its machine code, this allows the program as a whole to run in closer proximity to the machine. This means it requires less time for instructions to be executed; the instructions have less distance to travel to the main parts of the machine the program is running on. In addition, C++ also allows programmers to switch to assembly language or C at any point. This benefit is thanks to the language's backwards compatibility with C. The same goes for the relationship between C and C++. C is older, but it still proves useful to the functioning of the newer language, C++. In regards to performance, the last thing that C++ excels at is its ability to efficiently partner with other pieces of technology. This can be seen in how it pairs and communicates with various operating systems and hardware, as well as how it works with other languages to accomplish the task at hand. By allowing these various technologies to communicate with C++, the overall efficiency and simplicity of a program's performance is greatly improved.

On the opposite side of C++'s low-level features, it also offers the same high-level features that other strictly object-oriented programming languages offer. The difference between low-level features and high-level features lies in the

The Wii gaming platform is one place where C++ excels.

way the elements of the code function. If something is low-level in programming, it simply means that it functions much like the machine language used by the computer's processor does and requires little to no abstraction. To the human eye, low-level features appear clunky and nonsensical when written in code. High-level language features function more closely to how humans understand things, and do not rely on a specific type of machine in order to function, but can be implemented on a variety of computers. These can typically be read by programmers in a way that informs the programmer what that particular section of code is going to accomplish. Aside from inheritance and polymorphism (which define object-oriented programming), C++ contains additional characteristics that stem from this programming type.

Weaknesses of C++

Even though C++ is widely used today, it still has drawbacks. The largest weakness of C++ is its steep learning curve. Because it started out as a solution to a problem (which included solving Simula's lack of object-oriented design), it becomes increasingly more complex as it develops to new standards. In addition, it lacks the ability to manage memory like other object-oriented programs do. This means that C++ does not have a way to explicitly make or destroy objects and classes after they have been made. It is hard for newcomers to the language to grasp this concept since users often have to hardcode, or start from scratch, and create a **garbage collection** system to handle pieces of code that are no longer needed. Along with this, C++ has very specific syntax that must be followed in order for the code to execute as it should. Syntax is the textual formatting of a program. All of these issues stem from the fact that C++ is a lower-level language. As the programmer gets closer to the machine in question, the language becomes increasingly hard for a basic user to understand. However, C++ is not impossible to learn. With enough practice, any newbie can become fluent in the language.

While C++ offers many features that other languages do not, there are a few it doesn't have that affect performance. In addition to the lack of memory management mentioned above, it also lacks reflection and introspection features. These terms simply mean that C++ is missing the ability to look at its own code during runtime. If it had this capability, the language could be used to detect errors and adapt a program as needed. Another feature that C++ is missing is message passing, which is needed for various methods to communicate with one another. Imagine a programmer has one method to calculate the density, or mass divided by volume, of a cube. In the same program, there is another method that determines the volume. The methods would need to communicate their respective values to one another to accurately calculate the density in question. Unfortunately, C++ does not allow for this communication. However, with the use of the C++ library, this problem, as well as the issue of memory management, can be easily addressed by incorporating previously developed methods to resolve these issues. More experienced programmers even view these perceived flaws as positives, since C++ gives so much low-level control to the coder, allowing them to determine the functionality of the program as a whole.

The final issue worth discussing lies within the security capabilities of C++. The most common security problem C++ faces is that of buffer overflow. Buffer overflow can be found when an input field is given a set length and the user purposefully goes beyond the limit. What does this mean for security? One example where this could cause issues is with passcode-locked smartphones. Most passcodes limit their users to a selection of four numbers. However, it is possible to repeatedly copy and paste numbers into certain lock screens until the lock screen function becomes too overwhelmed to run correctly. The resulting failure is known as buffer overflow. This gives the hacker access

An inexperienced C++ programmer can inadevertently leave code and information vulnerable. C++ does not automatically provide protections.

to the device and the information it houses. While buffer overflow can be remedied by various methods within the C++ library, people who are unfamiliar with C++ may forget to address these concerns. Thus, their programs are left vulnerable to attack. Like any programming language, there are positives and negatives in using each, and it is just a matter of comparing and determining which one is better for the task at hand.

C++ vs. Python

Having covered the pros and cons of C++ as a language, one might wonder how it stacks up to the other available programming languages. When compared to Python, it is easy to see circumstances where one language would be more beneficial to use than the other. The first notable difference between the two stems from the type of language each one is. Python is defined as an **interpreted language**, which means it does require compilation in order to run. By ridding itself of the need to translate its own code into machine-readable code, Python's overall complexity is lessened. It demands less from the machine it is running on. Python's simplicity also carries into the syntax, or textual setup, of the language. Compared to C++, Python's formatting is very simple in nature. Programmers first see this in Python's lack of a main method. Where C++ requires this central framework from which to run its code, Python chooses to accept any method as the primary method. Therefore, a program can start from anywhere within the code. Additionally, Python's individual lines of code are much more simplistic. Python does not require semicolons or curly brackets to define when a line of code or method, respectively, ends. By removing the excess text, the code is much more pleasing to the eye and is more understandable. Python also has only three different types of numerical variables (spam, longspam, and float), whereas C++ has six. Since there are fewer rules to remember with Python than there are with C++, Python requires less development time when making comparable programs. Where a program in C++ could take up to a year to fully develop, a similar program in Python would only take about two months. Why even use C++ then, if Python seems like the better option?

The answer to that question lies in the functionality of each programming language. While Python is much simpler and easier to understand, its abilities are limited because of its simplicity. In more complex programs, it is important to maintain the integrity of the variables in use. Because Python uses implicit typing, this integrity is compromised. Implicit typing is when a program does not specifically state what type of variable is tied with each identifier, it simply assumes. For example, for a numerical value named "Money" that is set to 1,879,030,222, Python would simply assume this to be a "long" variable. It's often convenient that Python makes intuitive leaps. Yet sometimes, Python's assumptions cause problems.

For that same variable named "Money" initially set to some numerical value, there could be another place in the program where "Money" is set to "a" and is then considered a char variable. This could disrupt calculations and create security vulnerabilities.

On the other hand, C++ uses explicit typing. Therefore, each variable type has to be defined when it is initialized. An int variable will remain an int variable; a string will remain a string. The information these explicitly typed variables contain may differ, but they will never change type. This increases the complexity of the language, but explicit typing has more benefit in everyday applications.

The final difference between the two languages is the demographics each caters to. Since it is understood with a large amount of ease, Python is a great language for beginning programmers to experiment with. It introduces individuals to coding without the added complexities and rules. There are also a lot of resources for those who are looking to learn Python, since it prides itself on being a great first coding language. Once an individual has mastered Python, it is much easier to transition over to more complicated languages, such as C++. As you can be see, these two languages are very different, but each has an important role in programming.

C++ vs. Java

While the difference between C++ and Python was obvious from the beginning, even languages that are both rooted in object-oriented design, such as C++ and Java, can have some important differences. The first difference between the languages becomes clear when setting up a file to code in. Java requires a strict relationship between its filename and individual class names. This means that if a class is referred to as MedianFinder, the filename it is housed in must have the same name, down to the capitalization. C++ does not enforce such a standard, and it can even be seen as poor practice within the language to name things with a similar convention. Alternatively, because of Java's naming requirement, every piece of a Java program has to be part of a class. If there is not a class, there is not something to name the file it is in. To facilitate this system of organization, Java also implements **packages** within its program structure. Packages serve as a place to house multiple classes for a single program. They are similar to the folders found on a computer; they simply serve as a storage place. Conversely, C++ has a very loose organization structure that can be as strict or messy as the programmer desires.

Another key difference between the two is the presence of an automatic garbage collection system.

How Do They Compare?

○ ○ ○

With all this talk of simple versus complicated code, it's helpful to look at how these two languages really stack up against one another. In the example below, both languages are accomplishing the same thing, which is evaluating a simple xy calculation.

C++ Code:

```
int pow(int x, int y) {
int result = 1;
for (int i = 0; i < y; i++) {
result *= x;
}
return result;
}
```

Python Code:

```
def pow(x, y):
return x**y
```

The Python code seems easier to understand. The C++ code has to thoroughly outline the process of calculating a power function by multiplying the base number by itself within what's called a "for loop." A for loop is a simple coding structure that repeats until a certain parameter is met. In this case, "i" is no longer smaller than "y," as seen in the "i < y" check within the "for" loop definition. On the flip side, the Python code is able to do the calculation without extra effort.

As discussed in the weaknesses section, C++ does not currently have one of these systems in place. Java, on the other hand, does. This means that any object that is no longer being used within a program can be destroyed, allowing the memory space to be released and reassigned to something that would make better use of it. In this way, Java can be seen as more efficient. However, C++ is able to make the necessary accommodations to accomplish this as well.

Lastly, both languages have an extensive library in place to support their users. While neither is usable within the other language, a lot of the functionality of both Java's and C++'s library systems overlaps. Therefore, programmers using each language are asking the same things of Java and C++. Yet even though each language may be being used for similar tasks, the differences between the two are enough to make them separate entities. C++ is a lot like flying an aircraft, whereas Java is like driving a car. An aircraft needs more pieces than a car to work.

Just like an airplane has a lot of moving parts, C++ has many pieces that go into making functional code.

The Building Blocks:
A Look at C

It is no secret that technology is constantly building upon itself. Fire led to candles; candles led to lanterns; lanterns led to electricity. Much in the same way, typewriters led to computers, computers led to programming languages (like C), and C led to improved languages. One of those improved languages was C++. In fact, many aspects of C++ evolved out of C.

It should come as no surprise that because of the ancestral connection between the two, C++ is the only language that is backwards compatible with C. This compatibility helped as experienced C programmers transitioned over to the new and improved C++ coding language. In its prime, C was one of the more prevalent language options due to its easy-to-use Application Programming Interfaces (APIs), as well as its extensive compiler support. Due to its compiler support, C could be implemented on nearly any machine. While C++ continued this trend of portability, there are also a few key qualities that Stroustrup built upon to make C++ better than its predecessor.

At the most basic level, C++ has more features than C. C++ allows users to define strings in three different ways, whereas C only allowed for one. C++

How Java and C++ Work Together

○ ○ ○

Even though they are similar, both Java and C++ have their own individual uses in the tech world. One of those uses is the programming of various cellular devices. Android users can thank Java for their phone's capabilities. As for iOS users, they can thank C++. However, these programming requirements create some issues. A lot of companies develop applications for each mobile operating system! It requires a lot of money and time to constantly develop apps and their updated versions in two different programming languages. Consistency is extremely important for user experience, and there should not be any discrepancies between what is seen on the Android version versus what is seen on the iOS version of the same app. There is a solution: SWIG.

SWIG stands for the Simplified Wrapper and Interface Generator. It's what allows C++ to be used on a predominantly Java-run system found on any Android device. At the most basic level, all core code will be in C++. SWIG is then used to "wrap" the Java code

At their most basic level, Android devices run on C++.

around this input file and make it readable to the Android operating system. The process is started by running the SWIG command, which will separate any C++ classes into individual pieces, and generate a filename to match (recall the Java package system discussed earlier). These wrappers are then used to translate the C++ parts into things that Java will understand. Ironically enough, there is little functionality to the Java pieces of code. They merely serve as a means of translation from C++ into something Android can understand. With the help of the Java Native Interface, or JNI, Java code can be used by other languages and access their respective libraries.

Aside from Java, SWIG can be used to connect C++ to other languages including Javascript, PERL, PHP, Python, and Ruby. Originally written in 1995, this interface compiler has seen many updates and multiple editions, with the most recent one being released in 2017. In addition to serving as an interpreter between C++ and other languages, it is also useful in prototyping and debugging, systems integration, and constructing extension modules. While it is an incredibly useful tool to the C and C++ community, one of its weaknesses lies in the fact that it only caters to that specific programming language and cannot be used to translate other languages.

also allows variables to be declared anywhere within the program, another huge improvement that led to a more logical flow in calculations. Another important addition to C++ was the ability to overload functions. This meant that there could be multiple methods with the same name that would function in a certain way based on what type of input it was receiving. C++ also allowed for dynamic memory, with the simple addition of the keywords "new" and "delete." While it still did not have automatic garbage collection, like Java, these words could be used in much the same fashion

Knowing all the parts of C++ code allows you to create a strong, protected program.

If a new variable was to be created, it was prefaced with the word "new." Delete worked in the same way. Lastly, C++ incorporated classes and object-oriented programming, which allowed for a greater amount of flexibility.

When Should C++ Be Used?

Considering all that has been discussed in this chapter, the big question remains: So when should C++ be used? The answer depends on a few different factors. Based on the requirements of the program in question, the answer may change. However, at the most basic level, C++ should be used when performance is crucial. Its ability to work in close contact with the hardware it is running on allows for efficiency that would likely go unmatched if a programmer decided to use another language. In addition, the increased flexibility and control that it gives to the programmer makes C++ the perfect tool to be shaped into whatever is needed at the time. Another factor to consider is if the task at hand has a previous code base. If old versions of the program have already been coded using C or C++, it would not make sense to waste the time and money on coding it in an entirely new environment. Finally, if the programmer leading the project already has extensive experience in C++, that should be used to their benefit. C++ is a hard language to grasp, and anyone who can fully command its potential should make use of that knowledge. All in all, it's best practice to determine what the client, programmer, and program itself bring to the table; evaluate the options; and make the choice that makes the most sense for the task in question.

```
* FROM image_date ORDER BY shot_date DESC");

)) {

y("SELECT DISTINCT(studio) as studio, COUNT(*) as count FROM image WHERE day_id = '    ->id' AND
:fetch(          )) {
ay_info(    ->shot_date,           ->studio,"quick");
ray("studio" =>          ->studio, "count" =>           ->count, "title" =>          ->title

      ;
    ;

  , $studio) {

       )) die("error studio");

hot_date = '    '")     die('date not found');

image.id as image i         ge, image_date WHERE image_date.id=image.day_id AND image_date.shot
   )) {
e::get_copyright(          e_id);
get_models(     ->im
   ;

           on day_list() {

           ("SELECT  fr
```

Getting Started

O nce you've mastered the common terms that are used throughout the C++ coding community, you are poised to learn to code. At this point, technological requirements come into play. This chapter provides information about those requirements, describes resources for learning C++, examines career prospects for programmers, and looks at the latest implementations of the language.

Opposite: With all the available resources out there today, learning the code can be very easy.

Getting Yourself and Your Computer Ready

Since standard computers are not generally preloaded with an **integrated development environment (IDE)**, downloading one is where any new programmer begins. An IDE is the Microsoft Word of programming; it is where everything gets written, or in this case, coded. Within the C++ community, some popular IDEs are CLion, Visual Studio, and Eclipse. For beginning coders, Code::Blocks is a viable option—it can work with nearly any compiler, and it is free to the general public. In combination with an IDE, you must also download a C-/C++-compatible compiler. As previously mentioned, the compiler is what translates the code into machine-readable language and allows the program to execute on the device.

Once the terms have been learned and the technology has been installed, it is time to actually code! The next step in learning C++ is to explore the resources available. There are plenty of options out there to help people learn this language. Finding one is a matter of personal preference. Perhaps a hardcopy of a coding book would be most helpful. Or maybe a video tutorial on YouTube that walks its viewers through a program, step-by-step, would work better for your learning style. It might even be worth seeing if there are coding classes within the local community. Recently, there has been a push to get more people coding, so finding an option that works best for learners of all kinds and abilities is really an easy task.

Having gotten a handle on the basics of the language, there are a few things to remember throughout the learning process. It is important when completing tutorials not to simply copy and paste code into the IDE, but rather, understand what is happening and how the program works—although it may be beneficial to copy the code initially, to ensure that it works correctly and you understand what the goal of the program is. Beyond that, however, start thinking in the mindset of a programmer and refrain from simply copying the answer. If there is something you don't understand, there are numerous options designed to help and to answer questions. The internet is full of discussion boards and videos answering common, and not-so-common, questions about C++ code. Joining an online community will also provide opportunities to examine other programmers' code and to see how others solve the same problems in a multitude of ways. Finally, new and experienced programmers alike should not simply code tutorial exercises, but rather investigate real-world problems that they could solve with C++. There are any number of problems today that could be solved with the help of code.

Honing Your C++ Skills

While sitting down and physically coding in the language is the primary part of learning a new programming language, there are also other skills that can make learning C++ easier. Think of it like an athlete thinks of training. A runner doesn't simply run every day to make them the best marathon competitor. Many runners incorporate yoga to increase dexterity and lift weights to improve muscular endurance. Just as an athlete has a broad training plan to improve their specific skillset, so should an individual learning to code.

And luckily, you are already learning a variety of subjects in school. Formal education is a great starting point, and it is very easy to find classes that will help you make progress programming. Perhaps you're already familiar with algorithms from math class. Algorithms are mathematical equations that receive some variety of input, and then in turn, produce an output value. They can be something as simple as $x2$ or as complicated as the **Risch's algorithm**. Just like a program, an algorithm is made up of a variety of parts. If you understand how each part of an algorithm works, you can apply the same principles to programming. Aside from algorithms, many other mathematical concepts can strengthen a programmer's skills.

Classes like discrete mathematics, economics, and statistics complement coding skills. Not only do these classes foster computational thinking, but they also incorporate data analysis and research methodology. Learning to analyze data and developing a strong foundation in research methods is beneficial for anyone who wants to pursue a career in the technology sector.

Outside of formal schooling, there are a few notable options to expand programming knowledge. Open-source projects are one such resource. Open-source projects are projects that make the source code available to anyone who

GitHub helps coders around the world collaborate on projects.

wishes to collaborate on a piece. The term "open source" is just what it sounds like; source code that can be viewed by anyone. These types of projects allow a programmer to work with people of all skill levels and backgrounds on problems with varying levels of difficulty. Anyone can find a project that they feel comfortable contributing to and get their name added to the credits upon completion of the program. Participation in open-source projects also introduces coders to real-world applications of their code. And finding a project to join is easy. Quite possibly the most popular website for open-source work is GitHub. GitHub is a database for people to upload their projects, outline their needs, then find developers to assist in solving their problems. Their program gets completed, and programmers gain more experience. It's a win-win for everyone involved.

Another option for learning C++ is to become formally certified. The C++ Institute offers formal courses, examinations, and certifications for those interested in developing a more structured understanding of C++. Becoming certified means that an individual has successfully passed tests on a variety of topics related to the language, and they are up to industry standards. Not only does the process of certification allow an individual to learn and validate their skills, but it also makes them more desirable on the job market.

Important Non-Programming Skills

While technical skills are extremely important in learning C++, there are other professional skills to master to become the best programmer you can be. Strong communication skills are chief among the qualities that set the most successful programmers apart. In many workplaces, programmers are notorious for being poor communicators. Whether this is a fair characterization or not, recruiters are always impressed by programmers who speak and write effectively. Speaking skills are an important piece of programming for a few different reasons. First, programmers must be able to explain their code to a variety of different audiences. The way in which a programmer speaks to a CEO about a program would likely be completely different than how they would approach the same conversation with a fellow programmer. People within the technology sector will often be given tasks by those who do not understand coding, and knowing how to speak about complex functionality in a way that is easy to follow is a necessity. Additionally, programmers must be good at speaking publicly, as they may be expected to present their programs to those within their company and sometimes even to large, global audiences at conferences or product launches. Lastly, by verbalizing their process, coders can better explain why they made a particular design choice (for example) and validate their reasoning.

Writing is equally important. Writing can be required in any step of the development process from initial idea to final product. Programmers often do not work alone, so effective written communication can make this process easier on everyone involved. Emails regarding task delegation need to make sense, schedules need to be accurate, and questions need to be answered efficiently. This need can be seen in various settings, including GitHub projects, as they often connect developers from all over the world to work on a single project. In addition to the writing needed during collaborative endeavors, formal documentation also plays a large role in any tech project. Upon completion of a program, a formal document outlining the various elements, goals, and functions of a program must be described in understandable detail. These published writings need to be done correctly and in a way that people can understand.

To go along with communication, a programmer should also develop logic and time management skills. By thinking logically, programmers will be able to use abstract ideas to develop a program. Logical thinking can be sharpened through mind-based games, such as chess, sudoku, or mah-jongg. As for time management skills, these are important since programming projects are often given deadlines that must be met. While it may not take three weeks to create a program, within that three weeks, there must also be debugging, efficiency checks, and time allowed for overhead problems, such as issues with device performance. Without these skills, a company could face massive amounts of money lost, since the longer a program is in development, the greater the budget required.

Chess can help hone logic skills, no computer needed.

Job Prospects in C++

Because C++ is one of the most dominant programming languages in use today, there are many career options available to someone looking for a professional position. While it is not impossible to secure an entry-level job without some sort of secondary education, most positions require an associate's degree or higher in order to be considered. Upon successful completion of a degree, there are many career options to choose from.

Software Developer

One popular option for those wishing to program in their job is that of a software developer. Software developers are the individuals responsible for developing the various parts of a program. This includes developing the code and exploring the background functions that need to be completed in order for the program to execute. Software developers can be found contributing to any step of the program development process including writing, debugging, testing, and designing. In addition to creating and ensuring that the code is functional, software developers can also be found creating Graphical User Interfaces (GUIs). GUIs are the simplified menus that the average user would see, such as a start menu for a computer game. According to the US Bureau of Labor Statistics, jobs within software development are expected to grow as much as 17 percent by 2024, which would result in an additional 186,600 positions within the field. As of 2016, a software developer in the United States could expect to make around $49 per hour, or $102,280 a year. Based on experience and specialty, some software developers even make upwards of $160,000 a year.

The path to such an impressive salary begins with education. A potential software developer should hold a bachelor's degree in computer science, software engineering, or mathematics. For more desirable positions, a master's degree would also prove beneficial. In addition to education, experience should be completed during schooling, in the form of an internship or other entry-level position within the technology sector. From there, a software developer should sharpen their analytical, communication, and interpersonal skills to be the most ideal candidate for a position.

While the pay and other benefits are definitely a positive to this type of position, there are a few downsides that potential applicants should be aware of before committing to this career path. One of them is the limitation of one's location. There are software development jobs across the globe, but there are certain areas where the job market is more saturated with available positions than others. As of 2016, nearly 91 percent of available software developer jobs were located near Silicon Valley, California. This is not surprising, since Silicon Valley is home to Google, Apple, and Cisco Inc., to name a few. Other than California, open jobs center around larger cities, including Seattle, New York, and Dallas. Aside from

Software development is just one of the career paths that knowledge of C++ can lead to.

location, another consideration is the hours that the job requires. Oftentimes, software developers are expected to put in long hours, sometimes around eighty hours a week. Rigorous work schedules stem from the fact that some projects have short turnaround times and need to be completed quickly, regardless of the effort required from developers. While these cons may deter some, the promise of great compensation and a challenge from their job makes for a desirable career.

Game Developer

Another appealing option for those who are looking for a career that uses C++ can be found within the gaming industry. While game developers are considered to be a subset of software developers, the requirements of the game development positions vary. More commonly referred to as applications software developers, the duties of a game developer are far more creative and interactive than those of a software developer. Game developers are expected to collaborate with writers in generating storylines and character biographies. In addition, they document the game design process and develop prototypes for their teams. At the most basic level, game developers create the essential features of a video game. Just like software developers, game developers are expected to have a bachelor's degree in computer science, software engineering, or the like. However, it would also benefit an individual if they supplemented their major with more graphics-based classes, such as those incorporating Photoshop or 3D design software, like Maya. As of 2016, a game developer could expect to make about $100,000 a year.

After having decided to pursue a career in game development, there are a few things to consider. The first one is what type of **developing firm** an individual would like to work for. The most common types within the industry are first-party, second-party, and third-party development firms. First-party developers are those that manufacture a specific video game console and then produce games that work exclusively on that system. An example of this would be Nintendo, since Nintendo only produces games for its own consoles. A second-party developer is one that typically only produces for one console that they are contractually tied to (but they may branch out). Game Freak and its production of the *Pokémon* series is an example of this, since they typically produce games for Nintendo-based products but are not prevented from completing other projects. Third-party development projects are owned by companies outside of those that produce gaming

Writing and developing gaming software can be a viable career for those who are fluent in C++.

consoles. The very first company of this nature was Activision, which was founded in 1979. With each type, there are varying degrees of creativity and control that may be increased or lessened based on the project in development.

Though it may sound cool to work on video games as a career, there are some key negatives to game development that are worth looking at. The hours are often long and stress is usually high within these jobs, since there are tight deadlines to be met. In addition, there is a lot of potential for failure, as financial expectations may not be met or the gaming community may publicly bash the quality of the work put into a new game. However, this job would allow an individual the freedom to work on games every day and make them better, which not many people can say.

Technical Writer

People often believe that once an individual becomes well versed in a programming language, the only jobs available to them would be the ones that require they code. This is simply not true! Perhaps someone learned a programming language out of curiosity, and while they appreciate and understand it, they are not interested in devoting their time to a career that requires long hours and intense work environments. In this circumstance, a career as a technical writer might be a great fit. Technical writers are the individuals tasked with writing how-to guides, documentation for software and hardware, and scholarly journal articles that work to communicate difficult technical information to less technically experienced readers. It is not necessary to have a college degree in computer science, but a degree of some kind (usually in writing or English) is required. In addition, an aspiring technical writer should have some prior experience within the technology sector. As for pay, technical writers can expect to make around $33.58 an hour, with median annual pay landing around $70,000 per year. Job growth is not expected to skyrocket like software developers will see, but at a projected 10 percent increase by 2024, this is still a great field to get into!

In addition to writing, those in technical writing positions can also expect to study products, survey customers, and select from various mediums in which to convey their information. Because of this, technical writers can also benefit from more creatively driven courses, since they are expected to deliver text through interesting means online and through social media. These positions often do not require the long hours that development jobs may, but there is usually a need to accommodate those in other time zones. This could translate into an early or late workday. However, the lessened amount of stress and need to only work the normal requirements of a full-time job, while incorporating their previously acquired knowledge of coding, may make technical writing appealing to those who do not want to be programming on a regular

A technical writing career can be a good fit for tech-savvy individuals who do not want to code.

basis. Interestingly enough, those wishing to break into this field can receive certification just like their C++ inclined counterparts. Aside from the obvious skill of writing, technical writers should also have a good imagination, the ability to work with others, and technical skills.

New Technologies Using C++

While C++ has many everyday applications, the industry where it gets the most use is the video game industry. Unsurprisingly, then, the newest technologies incorporating C++ are found within game development software and gaming consoles.

Unreal Engine 4.15

The Unreal Engine 4.15 was released in early 2017. For those unfamiliar with game development, the Unreal Engine is a **video game engine** that was originally released by Epic Games on July 1, 1998. Since then, it has gone through three primary editions, and current releases are updates to its fourth edition. Unreal Engine 4 is a suite of integrated tools that allows game developers to create games, all while using C++ source code for the entire engine.

While Unreal Engine 4 was a great improvement to the previous editions, the most recent update in particular has given game developers a whole lot

Working Outside of an Office: A Look at Freelancing

○ ○ ○

Most professionals sit behind a desk, from at least 9:00 to 5:00, five days out of the week. However, for those people who want a little more freedom in their schedule and work environment, freelancing is a great option. Freelancing is when an individual takes on various projects from hiring individuals or companies, rather than working for a single company on a regular basis. For someone pursuing this type of career, finding consistent freelance work can be a challenge.

While securing freelance jobs can present difficulties, there are many resources and techniques that can lead to a successful career. The first resource is the internet: there are a number of sites that promote freelance work and help connect freelancers with those looking to hire. In addition, even job boards geared toward corporate jobs often have postings about contracted positions that require the flexibility of a freelancing employee. Additionally, varieties of self-promotion can come in handy when looking for freelance work. It is important to have an accessible online portfolio for potential employers to view past work and to provide contact information. Having a website for showcasing skills is only half the battle, however. In order to be effective, this website has to be viewed! In-person networking can help because it leads to name recognition. If a person's contacts hear of someone looking for a freelance programmer, there is a strong likelihood that they will suggest the person they know. Therefore, attending networking events can open up a variety of opportunities. Once a job is secured, a recommendation from that employer can be enough to create a consistent flow of work for freelancers.

Freelancing can give people the freedom they want in their own life, while still earning them a salary that can pay the expenses they accrue. As it stands right now, an individual who lands consistent work through freelancing can earn anywhere between $57,000 to $75,000 a year. According to Glassdoor.com, some people have even reported earning upwards of $150,000 while they are working from home and creating their own schedule! The current selection of C++ programmers listed on Upwork, one of many freelancing websites, charge anywhere from $20 to almost $60 an hour for their skills. The amount of income a freelance programmer generates depends on the motivation of the programmer to connect with others and generate work, their skill level, and their flexibility. Freelancing can be a great way to earn money and still have the freedom to live an exciting life, but there are drawbacks to this career path.

Although being in a cubicle forty hours a week may seem unappealing, there are some things that corporate life offers that freelancing cannot. The first is a consistent stream of income. Unless someone is fired or laid off, they can rely on their paycheck being deposited into their bank account on a regular basis. With freelancing, especially for those just starting out, there will be highs and lows to earning potential. Freelancers have to devote time and energy to acquiring work and building a client base for future projects. Because of this ebb and flow in income, freelancers often work on community-based projects in their less-busy work periods, so as to sharpen their skills and continue to put forth marketable work. In

Working Outside of an Office:
A Look at Freelancing
(continued)

○ ○ ○

Freelance work provides individuals with a lot of freedom to do what they like most, but it still requires a lot of work to maintain a client base.

addition to inconsistent work, freelancing lacks the standard benefits that come with most full-time jobs. Freelancing individuals must provide their own health insurance and start their own retirement savings plans, and they receive no paid time off. This often leads to freelancers charging more than an in-house programmer would, since freelancers have to balance these costs as well as receive adequate compensation for the work they put forth. Even so, for the right individuals, pursuing work through freelancing may create a highly satisfying lifestyle.

of new features to look forward to. **Compile times** for programs have been greatly lessened, cutting them by as much as half in certain instances. These shorter times are possible for a few different reasons. First, every header within the C++ code includes the necessary information to compile. They also include

The newest implementation of Unreal Engine has dramatically improved the graphics quality in the video games that are built using it.

only information to the other headers they need. This **Include What You Use (IWYU)** methodology lessens overhead within the program, allowing it to run faster. While the coding side of things has been improved, those focused on graphics also reaped many benefits with this release.

Unreal Engine users who are more graphically inclined saw a multitude of new features that would make their designs easier to implement. Improved texture streaming has been added, which reduces CPU usage and load times. This is useful for high-quality environments that are developed but then run on devices that cannot handle the original memory-intensive versions. This Automatic Memory Budgeting determines which materials within the gaming world need to be reduced while still maintaining the visual integrity of the game. The new edition also saw updates made to animation capability, material editing, and user interface options, to name a few.

While all the other features it added were great additions, quite possibly the most influential one was compatibility with the Nintendo Switch. Unreal Engine 4.15 allows its users to develop and release games that can be played on the Nintendo console that premiered in 2017. This feature was first deemed as "experimental" in nature but will switch over to a "shippable state" with coming updates. Going hand-in-hand with the Unreal Engine, the Nintendo Switch also relies on C++.

Nintendo Switch

Hitting markets worldwide on March 3, 2017, the Nintendo Switch was a highly anticipated release

The Wii U is just one of many technologies that uses C++ code. The Nintendo Switch (also coded in C++) was developed after the Wii U failed commercially.

within the video game industry. Nintendo developed this new gaming console to serve as a hybrid between portable and home consoles after the failure of the Wii U. Complete with a docking station for at-home use and Joy Con joysticks for portable play, the Switch has brought about a new way of gaming. This was an important event within the C++ community as well, since a majority of the titles released previously through Nintendo were partially or completely coded using C++.

As it stands, most users agree that the Switch has great potential, since Nintendo has paired up with Epic Games to allow for **indie developers** to make games. However, there are only 185 games available for the Switch as of this writing, which includes the long-anticipated *Zelda: Breath of the Wild*. In comparison, Xbox One features nearly 1,100 titles and the Playstation 4 has 1,594 games for its users to choose from. While the number of games will likely increase as time goes on, the success of the console may solely depend on how many game developers decide to create titles that are compatible with the new system.

Bringing It All Together

Bjarne Stroustrup's language has come a long way since its first standardization in 1998. It's hard to believe that such an important programming language had humble beginnings as a descendent of the Simula language and from Stroustrup's motivation to develop programming features for his thesis project. This general-purpose programming language sought to meet the demands of the programmer, making it an adaptable and useful tool to the programming community. Through its backwards compatibility with C and its influence on languages that were developed after it, C++ has had a lasting effect on the technology of today. While it may not be an easy language to learn, its towering presence makes it a beneficial tool worth mastering. With learning opportunities present in formal settings, such as schools, to more casual settings, such as online video seminars, learning C++ is possible for just about anyone. Whether someone takes on its steep learning curve or not, they have surely experienced C++ in one form or another.

From video games to various software applications, C++ is still thriving and taking the rapid changes of the tech world in stride. Because of this, there are many job opportunities available, from software developers to the less programming-intense positions, like technical writing. In addition to standard office jobs, C++ also allows the freedom for those individuals pursuing freelance work. Since it only requires a computer to develop code, C++ jobs can often be done anywhere. This, in combination with the growth of alternative career options, makes C++ a great choice for someone pursuing freelance work.

Work options aside, C++ has a large amount of potential for the future. Where other languages fade away because they've become obsolete within the technological sector, C++ continues to adapt to the broad needs of its audience. The future implementations that are slated to be released in coming years are direct proof. In addition to these updated standards, C++ and its ever-growing library of resources also contribute to its long-lasting usefulness to programmers. As long as Stroustrup and the C++ community keep adapting the language to their needs, it will surely be around for years to come.

abstraction The process by which a programmer or program filters out details to show only what is completely necessary for the functioning of the program.

backwards compatibility The ability to use a programming language or piece of technology that came before with a new language or technology.

classes Basic outlines of the methods and variables used with a program. A class serves as a template to objects.

compile time The time it takes a compiler to translate a program into machine-readable code and check for potential errors.

constructor The part of the class that actually builds an instance of an object. This is the part of the code that defines what variables will be available in the newly created object.

data structures The structures that allow for program information to be organized and stored. These can be made from trees, lists, and arrays.

debuggers A program that can assist the programmer in finding errors and complications within the code.

developing firm The formally organized company that develops, publishes, and distributes a particular video game.

directive The lines of code that are read during the preprocessing of a program. Directives tell the compiler how to prepare itself for the incoming program by informing it of the various library files that may be used within the program.

embedded systems A computer system with a defined use, such as computers developed solely for financial banking or airline booking.

extensions Add-ons made available to a program or implementation of a programming language.

functions A collection of statements within the program that perform a particular task.

garbage collection A form of memory management that automatically deletes methods that are no longer being used. C++ does not automatically provide this, but it may be programmed to accommodate such memory deletion.

Include What You Use (IWYU) The idea that a program should only include what it uses within its code, so as to avoid unnecessary lines of code.

indie developers Independent video game developers who release games on their own, without help from big corporations.

integrated development environment (IDE) A software application that provides various tools to make programming easier, such as inline code suggestions and a simplified view of the debugging process.

interface The application that allows a user to communicate with a computer, or what a user sees when a program is run.

interpreted language A programming language that does not require compilation, or translation of its source code to machine-readable code, like Python.

kernel The part of the computer that holds the core computing power, known as the operating system.

method A programmed section of a class that is meant to accomplish something for the program.

object A particular instance of a class that holds specific information to that iteration of the object in question.

object-oriented programming (OOP) A variety of programming that implements objects within its code.

package A collection of Java classes housed together, often in a .JAR file.

Risch's algorithm A complicated algorithm used within computer science.

scripting The process of generating web pages on the internet.

standardization The process of developing and recognizing the various rules of a programming language as the de facto version and having clear guidelines laid out by an organization regarding the specifics of a language.

subsidiaries The term used to describe a company that is operated by another company, such as the relationship between Lucent Laboratories and Nokia.

syntax The rules determining how keywords, phrases, and symbols work together within a program, similar to how grammar controls the English language.

video game engine A software package used to design and develop video games.

zero-level abstraction The lowest form of abstraction in a program, meaning the code has little to no details provided. (See "abstraction.")

Books

Dawson, Michael. *Beginning C++ Through Game Programming.* 4th Edition. Boston: Cengage Learning, 2014.

Lippman, Stanley, Josee Lajoie, and Barbara E. Moo. *C++ Primer.* 5th Edition. Upper Saddle River, NJ: Pearson Education, 2013.

McGrath, Mike. *C Programming in Easy Steps.* 4th Edition. Warwickshire, UK: In Easy Steps Limited, 2012.

Stroustrup, Bjarne. *Programming: Principles and Practice Using C++.* 2nd Edition. Upper Saddle River, NJ: Pearson Education, 2014.

Websites

LearnCPP

http://www.learncpp.com

Explore an extensive list of lessons that cover a wide array of topics within the C++ coding language.

SoloLearn

https://www.sololearn.com/Course/CPlusPlus/

SoloLearn's C++ lesson plan provides nine different modules about C++ to choose from, with quizzes to test your new skills.

TechRocket

https://www.techrocket.com/code/c++-courses

The TechRocket website provides C++ coding materials in fun, interactive, and game-like lessons.

Udemy

https://www.udemy.com/courses/development/programming-languages/C-plus-plus-tutorials/

Udemy offers rated lessons, both free and fee-based, that allow users to learn in whatever way best suits them.

Videos

C++ Programming with Derek Banas

https://www.youtube.com/watch?v=Rub-JsjMhWY

This hour-long video introduces the C++ coding language, complete with in-video examples and additional materials to better your understanding.

C++ Programming with LearnVern

http://www.learnvern.com/course/c-programming-tutorials/

LearnVern's video lecture series outlines the C++ language with easy-to-follow examples and understandable C++ programs to code along with.

Bingul, Ahmet. "Advantages of C++ over C (for Teaching)." Report, University of Gaziantep, May 2009.

Bjork, Russell C. "A Comparison of the Syntax and Semantics of C++ and Java." Report, Department of Computer Science, Gordon College, 2003.

Bureau of Labor Statistics. "Software Developers." December 17, 2015. https://www.bls.gov/ooh/computer-and-information-technology/software-developers.htm.

———. "Technical Writers." December 17, 2015. https://www.bls.gov/ooh/media-and-communication/technical-writers.htm.

C++ Institute. "Frequently Asked Questions." Retrieved May 2, 2017. https://cppinstitute.org/faq.

Chopping, Dominic. "Nokia Sees 95% Ownership Stake in Alcatel-Lucent." June 16, 2016. http://www.marketwatch.com/story/nokia-sees-95-ownership-stake-in-alcatel-lucent-2016-06-16.

Computer History Museum. "Bjarne Stroustrup." Retrieved March 19, 2017. http://www.computerhistory.org/fellowawards/hall/bjarne-stroustrup/.

Cplusplus.com. "History of C++." Retrieved March 17, 2017. http://www.cplusplus.com/info/history/.

GitHub. "About." Retrieved May 2, 2017. https://github.com/about.

Glassdoor. "Game Developer Salaries." Retrieved May 2, 2017. https://www.glassdoor.com/Salaries/game-developer-salary-SRCH_K00,14.htm.

Indeed. "Freelance Programmer Salaries in the US." Retrieved May 2, 2017. https://www.indeed.com/salaries/Freelance+Programmer-Salaries,-United+States.

Meyers, Scott. "The Most Important C++ Software ... Ever." Artima Developer, August 23, 2006. http://www.artima.com/cppsource/top_cpp_software.html.

Nokia Bell Labs. "Timeline." Retrieved March 19, 2017. https://www.bell-labs.com/timeline/#/2010/1/closed/.

Python. "Comparing Python to Other Languages." Retrieved March 22, 2017. https://www.python.org/doc/essays/comparisons/.

Saylor Academy. "CS101: Introduction to Computer Science I." Retrieved March 19, 2017. https://learn.saylor.org/course/cs101#2.1.2.

Stroustrup, Bjarne. "Evolving a Language in and for the Real World: C++ 1991–2006." Report, Texas A&M University, 2007.

———. "Some Information about Bjarne Stroustrup." Retrieved March 19, 2017. http://www.stroustrup.com/bio.html.

———. *The Design and Evolution of C++*. Reading, Massachusetts: Addison-Wesley, 1994.

———. "The Essence of C++." Video. Edinburgh: The University of Edinburgh, May 6, 2014.

SWIG. "Executive Summary." May 29, 2016. http://www.swig.org/exec.html.

TutorialsPoint. "C++ Exception Handling." Retrieved March 22, 2017. https://www.tutorialspoint.com/cplusplus/cpp_exceptions_handling.htm.

Veerasamy, Jeyakesavan. "C++ vs. Java: Similarities & Differences." Presentation. Dallas, Texas: University of Texas. http://www.utdallas.edu/~veerasam/lectures/C++vsJava.pptx.

Waymo. "On the Road." Retrieved March 19, 2017. https://waymo.com/ontheroad/.

<Index/>

Page numbers in **boldface** are illustrations. Entries in **boldface** are glossary terms.

abstraction, 11
Amazon, 25
applications software developers, 86
assembly language, 17, 32, 56
AT&T, 11–12, 15
automatic garbage collection, 66, 72

bachelor's degree, 84, 87
backslash, 45–46
backwards compatibility, 26, 56, 69, 98
BCPL, 8–10
Bell Laboratories, 10–13, **11**, 15, 20. 28
Boolean, 36–37
Boolean constants, 40–41

C with Classes, 6, 10, 14, 16, 20–21
Cambridge University, 7, **7**, 9, 28
CFront compiler, 16–19
char, 37–38
character constants, 42
child class, 35
classes, 7–8, 23, 33–36, 60, 66, 70, 72
compiler, 14, 16–17, 19, 23, 69, 71, 76
compile time, 95
constructor, 59

data abstraction, 33
data structures, 22
debuggers, 18, 71, 82, 84
developing firm, 87
directive, 49

e-commerce, 25
embedded systems, 53
exceptions, 58–59
extensions, 26, 71

floating point types, 39
freelancing, 92–94, 99
functions, 22, 26, 35, 49, 57, 67, 72, 82, 84

garbage collection, 60, 66, 72
Google, 51–52, 85

Include What You Use (IWYU), 95
indie developers, 97
inheritance, 34–35, 57
integral variable, 38
integrated development environment (IDE), 76–77
interface, 25, 71, 96
interpreted language, 63

Java, 25, 66, 68, 70–72
Javascript, 71

kernel, 10

library, 22, 49, 59, 61–62, 68, 71, 99

method, 34–35, 37, 40, 48, 58–59, 61–64, 72, 79

Nintendo, 87, 96–97
numerical constants, 41
numerical variables, 64

object, 22, 26, 32–34, 60, 68
object-oriented programming (OOP), 24–25, 32–33, **32**, 35, 72
open-source projects, 79–80

package, 66, 71
parent class, 35
PHP, 71
polymorphism, 35, 57
portable implementation, 9
private object class, 34
protected object class, 34
public class, 34
Python, 63–67, 71

Risch's algorithm, 78
Ruby, 71
runtime, 8, 17, 59, 61

security, 22–23, 34, 61–62, 65

self-driving cars, 52–53

Simula, 6–10, 60, 98

smartphone, 5, 62

software developers, 24, 83–86, 99

special characters, 42, 45, 47

standardization, 29, 98

string constants, 42

string variable, 39, 59

Stroustrup, Bjarne, 6–10, 14–24, 26–29, **28**, 69, 98–99

subsidiaries, 11

SWIG, 70–71

syntax, 7, 17, 60, 63

technical writers, 89–91, 99

templates, 58

Unreal Engine, 91, 96

variable, 8, **9**, 36–40, 42–43, 46, 58–59, 64–65, 72

video game, **43**, **50**, 86–88, 91, **95**, 97, 99

video game developers, 86–88, 91, 98

video game engine, 91

Waymo, 52–53

zero-level abstraction, 8–9

Ashley M. Ehman graduated from Carroll University, where she studied information technology, professional writing, and graphic design. She currently lives in Madison, WI, where she is launching a freelance graphic design business. In her free time, she enjoys making computer-based 3D models, playing *Pokémon Go*, and traveling. To find out more about her or to see her most recent work, visit her website at http://www.ashleyehman.wordpress.com.